Here is my street,
this tree I planted

Copyright © Jonathan Bennett, 2004

Published by ECW PRESS
2120 Queen Street East, Suite 200, Toronto, Ontario, Canada M4E 1E2

All rights reserved. No part of this publication may be reproduced, stored in a retrieval system, or transmitted in any form by any process — electronic, mechanical, photocopying, recording, or otherwise — without the prior written permission of the copyright owners and ECW PRESS.

The characters, incidents, and dialogues are products of the author's imagination and are not to be construed as real. Any resemblance to actual events or persons, dead or living, is purely coincidental.

NATIONAL LIBRARY OF CANADA CATALOGUING IN PUBLICATION

Bennett, Jonathan, 1970–
Here is my street, this tree I planted / Jonathan Bennett.

Poems.
ISBN 1-55022-648-7

I. Title

PS8553.E534H47 2004   C811'.6   C2003-907293-2
A misFit book

Editor: Michael Holmes / a misFit book
Cover and Text Design: Darren Holmes
Production and Typesetting: Mary Bowness
Printing: Gauvin Press

This book is set in Goudy.

The publication of *Here is my street, this tree I planted* has been generously supported by the Canada Council, the Ontario Arts Council, the Ontario Media Development Corporation, and the Government of Canada through the Book Publishing Industry Development Program. **Canadä**

DISTRIBUTION
CANADA: Jaguar Book Group, 100 Armstrong Avenue, Georgetown, ON, L7G 5S4

PRINTED AND BOUND IN CANADA

Here is my street, this tree I planted

Jonathan Bennett

ECW PRESS

for Wendy

"I guess I am not very human. I didn't just want to paint people posturing and grimacing; what I wanted to do was to paint sunlight on the side of a house."

— Edward Hopper

Contents

Drive 1
Roman Road 2
After Hopper's *Early Sunday Morning* 3
Gunnamatta Bay 4
The Geopolitics of School Shoes 6
The Spider 7
Stripped Fitter for the Outing 8
The Dope 12
Measure Twice 13
Demolition at the CNIB 14
The New Normal 15
The Otonabee Poems 16
An Imprecise Outline 27
August Morning 28
August Afternoon 29
Widow's Walk 30
The Shore 31
Where Seagulls are Local 32
Via the Mine 41
The Price is the Price 42
Crowd of Two 44
A Confidential Morphology 45
Douglas Fir 46
Chelmsford Avenue 47
Black Cloth 48
Rain 49
Hostage Hostel 50
Here is my street, this tree I planted 51
Last Stand of the Wollemi Pine 52

Notes & Acknowledgements 58

Drive

The mind, a chatter of directions, ashtray
mediation. A junction of hard lefts,
rights, into a disappearance as if tail

light embers over the crest of a hill.
A mannish want to just drive. There are clouds.
Was there mention of weather, of work?

Something about the earlier meal lingers;
anticipation ended in a mouthful.
For now, threnody: her voice, injury.

The consoling roams in words, but weakly:
the thirsty coming upon dry riverbeds
wish for restoration, endless waters.

Dashboard blue, the consol as if conscious.
Over there, a strung tree (high as a reach)
flickers with cheery seasonal lights.

Roman Road

A Roman road, the Lancashire field impressed,
bruised, in an uneven, slight way
that might have been misattributed

by the uninitiated to weather, Victorian
plough, divine whimsy, historical slurry.
You surfaced this site for me, colonial boy,

as we sloped off home from the accident —
concussed, recalcitrant — our heads
full of coppers, mirror shards,

we hoisted over piled stone fences
rimming hills. The day, dank dusk,
grey cloud, a final blow to our chances,

found me humming something popular
to sluice out the ever-oncoming tractor,
the boom of my head against window,

your savage, double-clutched "no, no."
You get cool, older, busy. Guide me
by the arm, talk rugby, snooker,

female nous, Guinness, before stopping.
"There. That's Roman is that dip."
Two stocky slaves, bound, smash the fecund

paddock up ahead with crude, sour blows.
I watch. You walk on across the field to tell
your father his car hit a tractor on the road.

After Hopper's *Early Sunday Morning*

                      And so you begin
to populate the town like this,
force stories through each curtain slit,
shove lives into the idea of rooms.

This pleases you — as if a real estate agent,
or a Private Dick with some agency —
as does the lone shadow, how it marks
the pavement where you loiter kerbside.

The town. This idea of town, at dawn,
surrendering to the flawless vacancy of it,
romanced by the depressive era dust —
or the hydrant on the lip of the kerb, there

just so you will think how the composition
depends upon the barber's pole,
coloured in red, white and blue
on America's main street, with awnings;

citizens yawning in curtained apartments
above, consider coffee, or bathing,
or church, or just how to best use
                      their day of freedom.

Gunnamatta Bay

Of a morning he'd fire up the old red ute,
leg-up us two helpers in back with traps,
greasy chains, the missing rollick.
Take us out in the old trawler,

our early manhood ripening like
the garden's blood and bone, the bag
of mullet berley lashed to the skirting,
the old man's pipe-breath.

Red too was the boat, chugging,
the mechanical spluttering its way
through the aboriginal —
Gun-na-mat-ta, Gun-na-mat-ta,

before the sun got up we were off
down the coast a bit farther
than the bombora, far as
Wat-ta-mol-la, Wat-ta-mol-la,

tall tales of bream, blokes like
you've never — Trevally, Tailor,
Snapper, John Dory, Leatherjacket,
Wobbygongs. He'd pull the traps,

tip 'em up on the rolling deck,
the scene spilling alive with gasping,
fine-toothed mouths screaming
out their guts, but ancient alarm struck

in their lidless eyes, taken, bound above
the surface to bear witness: to our anti-life,
to terror itself, beyond the very edge
of a conceivable world — *Terra Australis*.

The place up over, from which falls wrecks,
drowning boys, traps set free to float the tides.

The Geopolitics of School Shoes

Clarks. That imperialist cobbler, pragmatic
and straight-laced gaoler of the broad
and beautiful brown and bare foot.

Shackled square-toed submission,
treadless agony at little lunch,
turning after-school footy into

a bloody bitumen-blistered rage.
You'd have sold your mother,
and her entreaties:

they let your feet breathe!
(As children it seemed we
were podiatric asthmatics)

for a pair of Dunlop Volleys,
your friend's KT 26ers:
all the power of a Holden V8!

Clarks. Scamper across the sand
and into the sea, the black weight
and raw heat of them cast away

on the shore like the harrowing
conditions of the English foreigners
for whom they were made.

And so, the day they arrived
breakdancing from America,
Nikes slid on with power, with fame,

you spoke of *dude* instead of *mate*,
far out not *reckon*, and run, well you'd
run as if someone new was cheering you on.

The Spider

Island ablaze, shore-bound audience abuzz.
Electric light trails, auburn star lick. Aflame.
Lake heat, lighting abyss: planes adjoin, agape.
Darkness outlining amber. Alarm, tears.
Women aghast. Men outboard, throttling.
(Later, sleep blisters, bursting open, raw.)

Clutches of morning coffees, a red canoe.
A child's ruddy cheeks, charcoal coarsened stand,
a conifer's alligator skin, baked.
Wet smoke rings, sooty, filth, the dissolving
array: a skeletal image, a pine
                              brittle in the rime.
There are hungers here, northward, silent, flawed.
The dog's muddy nose; a spider, its web anew.

Stripped Fitter for the Outing

"Well so long, Mister, till we meet again"

I

Park in the middle, strut a wavy radius
through cars owned by those more eager,

cross mounds of dung long ago belted down
(the back of a shovel) and overcome by turf.

Pockmarked terrain: deliberate steps.
Here is the hallowed racing turf itself.

I: the governance of small white men and fear,
the majority whip, and how as a horse I'd want

to vote with my feet, lose often and badly.
You: Did you ever see *Equus* performed?

The sun hot on the neck but wet underfoot,
the dew flicks a little on the shins, inside

three hundred and sixty degrees of furlongs
the white barrier rails, resonance, seconds:

everything is predictable and on-track.
Grass silk beautiful, the chances for us grow.

(There's an urge to bend, kiss it for luck.)
Hopes awash . . . the horses mate. Ah, yes! Go!

II

Across straw-covered sod an old-timer mans the gate,
directs late cars. Alcoholic nose, sun-scorched brow.

Two-up, pensions on rust-coloured schooners of beer,
bets misplaced on outlandish trifectas. You grimace.

(His arthritic finger, hooked so profoundly,
drivers disobey to avoid an adjacent van.)

Old soldiers. Singularities. Question-mark-bent
under a standard-issue grey felt hat, orange feather

snagged in the band, his father too, a lifetime ago.
You mutter about skin cancer, I wince at metastasize.

A significant woman clops past, flanked by others
in jodhpurs and blue sweaters from the country class.

A photographer jogs alongside to capture
this Dubbo-bound Marie de' Medici on her journey.

File through turnstiles, buy guides.
Beer, sweat, pipe tobacco, fried food, horse.

. . . *Short half-head . . . Racing in Brisbane*.
The bookie's ring in the grandstand's lee,

pavilions, inviting windows: "MIN. $1 BET"
in white letters on black signs where fathers

put fifty cents each way for sons.
Ya feel lucky, mate? You hold the ticket.

His winsome, underemployed smile
that as good as says: *I love you son.*

And hair is lightly mussed with knuckles
transmitting how this goes across generations.

III

Round the bend, *carn you bloody-b-ooty!*
up the straight, jockeys in crimson stars,

purple stripes, black and white checks crouched
above the saddle, *Give 'im a bit of it, Micko.*

The old digger again, his crooked finger, in charge
now of picking up rubbish cast among the seats.

Down the straight a jockey falls and the horse
just keeps going, nevertheless:

slick, dapple-grey mare, head back, fortunate,
charging toward home on her own terms.

The jockey escapes a trampling, dusts himself off:
a lone scarlet figure facing a long, slow walk.

The riderless horse (disqualified) wins.
I: Would you look at that! You: Is he hurt?

Can't hold 'em back, the old-timer says,
wandering off with his broom, hunting up

plastic cups, Mars Bar wrappers, spilt hot chips.
Father kisses son, their second is first.

Between races, from our grandstand height
we spot our car parked in the middle, our eyes

plot separate courses to it, wavy radii.
This is how we got here, this is how we shall go.

The Dope

*If there's the smell of dope at a party
then you know someone brought their parents —*

I'm telling her this light-heartedly, the way you talk
at lunch to co-workers. I order tuna on brown

and she lights up and I think sometimes her eyes
have been preserved, between bright blinks I catch

a snap of her at about my age, twenty-odd years ago.
Other times I think she's dying —

what else could explain why she tells me of every jean jacket,
ex-lover, Zeppelin song, California road trip, well-rolled

doobie, lousy mistake, faux-paint finish, trashy novel,
70s movie, store-top apartment, beloved dog, cool car,

shit job, friend she's ever lost,
                              lusted after, been betrayed by.

Measure Twice

The smell is cedar sawdust, the sound is dog.
Will he return to this summer again?
A flattened hand over the bared belly —
the thumping animation, a dogleg.
The skill saw's blade rests still on grass blades.
Overhead, its head, teeth bob at his mouth,
a tongue-flash to lick clean his beard, his face
hides the sun that illuminates errant clouds.

Oh, I am pinned on the grass, *Stopit!* —
helplessness can be welcome if framed.
Tomorrow, gold light, overexposed like
a dream: will it once again call to his
ill-judged frame? Or perhaps an inside out ear?
An abstruse oblong? Or simply an end, here?

Demolition at the CNIB

Hand outstretched for the wall's curvature dips
at the beep ahead, the t-junction whirrs
of dot matrix. Mind your mind. Inclined, railed,

then pine, lavender, voice: "Fragrant Garden
perennial bulb sale, five dollars a bag."
The guide dog, handle strapped at its back sits

under a cafeteria table,
ignoring the fat one's spilled fries, misplaced
heels at hopeful flies restrains its impulse

to swish its tail, or to bark, or get lost.
And what of the sign: "The Looming Ladies,"
on the door, far, far down the windowless

hallways, a relic, from the yesterdays
of sheltered workshops, other worlds now fingered.
No, don't forgive me as I grope along

confronting an imagined night mourning
its tactility, liberty, pity.
They rise up, shriek, dance among the flames.

Translate this hell into a pidgin Braille.
Make it ironic where you played it straight,
dark where light, touching on abandonment.

The New Normal

Another press conference and they speak slowly,
over-explain the contingencies,
choose words that mean exactly blamelessness,
tuck behind epidemiology,
or the Premier's lapel, and the news
runs pictures of masked throngs in the streets, or
chinamen poking at caged civet cats,
the brave mayor thumbs up local dim sum.

Am I falling in love with this new normal?
Its stop signs on the doors, mass quarantines,
its revocation of the right to touch
lips, break bread, shake hands, congregate, complain.
A streetcar rumbles along Dundas West.
It is the setting sun. It is the test.

The Otonabee Poems

I. Salamander

In that fractional space,
between thick belly
of rock and ripe earth,
you rest out the season.
You've endured worse —

lava, liquid fire, one hundred
million winters hidden after
past glaciers hack, dragged
roofs off your
                grandfathers' backs.

A helmetless torso, an edible
shorn tail for osprey and hawk.
Metamorphoses discarded
the uneconomical parts away,
added others, the remains

are a slick circumstance
on a voyage back to swamp, beginnings,
openings from frozen pools once teaming,
caught leaves, cryogenic nettles,
ice-clear cryptic wormholes.

The root cuts a line across
your private forest floor.
Such diagonal, unrelated
serpents rise and fall in
and through the mud until

it takes a dive sharp under
moss-encrusted stone.
A reappearance scheduled for elsewhere.

What ruddy work is to be done here?
What laborious days?

Such breaking operation to accomplish,
to colonize and fix a manifold presence
among rock and root and mud
and ice and leaf and hoof print,
faeces, twig, stick, stone, bone.

You can stare it down. Recreate it next year,
after a season or two passes and a tree melts
into the soil and a rainwater pool
snaps into ice over a moonless night
in mid-November. You can have it all

again, this grey canvas,
this accidental sculpture,
this found art. You can
call it your home, your love,
memory, country, your history —

you can call it into question.
No matter, afterwards you will forget
the elemental accuracy, the carbon,
that is present within this topography.
You will lose the sense of touch.

What remains is a projection,
a phantom memory,
an homage, what remains is
a replication of this, here,
this burden, this ancient silence.

II. Coyote

The amphitheatre rises,
a waterless fall of moss,
rock crop and tuft,
requires a moment

(that's understatement)
interrupts you,
this gully is track's end,
a front paw lifts

from the fallen leaf cover,
suspends twitches.
The rot, mulch, the return
of compounds so active

it all hums
about the pricked ears.
Suddenly the floor scrapes up,
the stillness of it snapped.

Imagining a crowd
of impossible characters,
how they ensemble around you.
This is not the big time:

only local production, operetta,
but you're the lead tenor.
Nostril steam, a string of saliva
hanging, chops engaged,

climb notes of scales
lost against the weather
bulk hard in here,
late light, conjecture

at the critic's absence,
what remains but the act,
the atmosphere,
the environs of woodwind

orchestrating deep
dense swaying
branches of cedar forest.
Rolling thunder, timpani

and the empty-eyed crowd
strikes a short breath
at your aria, its rise
to the sky heights, its climb,

hoist, its heroic potency.
This a steely afternoon
reserved for the foolhardy,
stalwart in the sudden whip

from the north, fall leaves lift,
play for effect, your song,
croon, cast cry, your howl,
becomes the shiver itself

and of course you revel for this
is destiny manifested singular.
This oral history, lost hunt,
the wait, gain, the fill, call,

a puff-chested sway
(was that a prance?)
then a great slow bow,
two shifts back, a pause,

a histrionic sigh, then
departure left: a stage,
littered with month-old leaf,
orange and brown.

Mongrel theatre, an installation
of the wild-gold radiant earth.

III. Deer

You, an almost buck, skating, hooves
eking out rock for traction. Does she still
sleep among the cedars, your clearing,
or is she gone now?

You twitch at the thought or else
the coldness here as the track opens
to a spot where fall rain pooled
in amongst loose stones, hardened one night.

Just like that for a night to hold things up now,
the way the water moved — implicated
in grey pallet, brush swirl, swish, and stroke.
Sure feet on blackened ice mean slow passage,

only a scent of her moves you on,
an inclination that this is what you
are supposed to do, a young man of your ilk,
to carry on and head right back to the place.

You sniff at how far this light wind has come
to accompany you on your way. It's like you,
that it knows where it's going because it's already there.
You follow along an olfactory map. Does she mean now?

You wonder at misgivings despite yourself,
imagining her now, in full, balking at the possibility
that all you will recover is her indentation, an outline
cast in the remaining snow as if the snow remembers

her too because the warmth from her melts the top crust
a little as she sinks into white sleep. She will have been there
if bronze touches of her fur remain, re-frozen
then ripped out as she stood up from her mould.

This then, if she did not wait while you fawned
over her, traversing the frozen ground.

IV. Great Blue Heron

From high
you see the endlessness
of the rock. But also how
it sometimes tucks neatly
under fir trees, or burnt
black pine, like it meant
to make the gully, a snag, first
for dirt, seagull shit, rotting leaf,
a sprout and then a lone pine grows
up to be a landmark, a point
of reference, before oddly,
mysteriously becoming charred.

From high
such a thoughtful move
looks artistic, intentional,
an aesthetic placement
by an exterior designer,
at the very least purposeful —
insofar as schemes matter.

Whereas from low
when you carve a parallel glide
for the whole length of the lake,
it's all about how and where
this rock is bare. As every piece,
each outcrop, lichen crusted
hunk, makes you brim
with homespun pride.

And what fat decadence
it is to land on an island of soft
grey and just perch a bit before
sunrise and look up at the clouds
rolling by in waves like sand banks
that undulate when you skim over shoal

and the shallow water. Not something
to do often but when the occasion
arises, when the reeds and shorelines
are loathsome, when no others
are looking, landing on such a lone slab,
the lake oscillating up against it
in small wet rhythms, is what gives flight
such purpose and definition —

Off again then
over the morning lake, the air
its own temperature and colour,
a safe nature outside, approachable
realism steeped with glory, captured
by flight, rimmed by primordial shell.

V. Small Canadian Boy

There's a rock that juts out into the lake
not far from your place, your place up north

so that when you run and jump you hang
in the sky, like time doesn't matter,

your arms whirling and your legs
kicking out, toes extended anticipating

the freezing water when it'll rush
up your body in a lickety-split instant,

but it hasn't happened yet, you're still falling,
forever, through the summer naked air

carrying the faint, gorgeous memory
of warm rock on the browning skin of your back,

and it lingers because the cold lake hasn't taken it
away in that flash, a splash, like school

when it smacks you, comes crashing back,
but no not yet — you will

this leap to last forever, forever
gliding up here towards the blue lake below,

maybe until you die, forever because the rock overhang
is not far from your place, your place up north, forever

because you broke your arm jumping
off it that summer, forever

because you kissed your friend's cousin behind it —
oh the girl with orange-crush lips, forever

because you looked up at the stars on it
that cool night under the blanket, forever

because you remain more like you near it
than any other place: the pink and grey rock

covered in those green dry moss flecks.
It will always be the one solid furnishing

in your world, unalterable, resolute,
like the bones of the earth.

An Imprecise Outline

You fry eggs and tell me of your dream,
the fish with the head of a dog and I think
about my mother's that passed last week.

For a final gift she gave him a collie pup —
gave it and left for good. A baby with a beard.
Then he left for Thailand and gave it right back —

Take that. So in the end it was hers.
The dog lasted ten years: an imprecise
outline of the way we got on with it —

before your strange dream, piling image
upon deviant image, restored us to ourselves.

August Morning

Around the bed the dog's tail circles — a periscope.
Looking for what, at this hour?
It is still much too early for cereal.
In Australia, they are on to aperitifs.
There is the state of the world
about which to worry, or work,
a book could be read, or written.

Now a dorsal fin, the curtain a jib — full on a tack.
Within stellar conventions, a mind
forgets its ideas. Gazpacho repeats.
How often should ducts be cleaned?
Up. First light pools in the ditch
sorting out goldenrod and thistle
from night's evening dimness.

A dog now: at a groundhog trespassing — civil yelp.
Purebreds, mutts: gerrymander apart.
Poets consider ethical investing, blood
diamonds, over port. Pathetic. Fallacious.
Been years since the intelligentsia
noted petit bourgeois acts. A branch
fallen in the garden. Lightning?

Cornflakes. Juice. Read nothing into it — faux gravitas.
This is countryside with no allusions.
This is daytime with people employed.
This is the epoch of bullet points.

August Afternoon

Beyond the bulrushes corn advances,
ears to the sky in concentrated march,
roll down the hills, down to Rice Lake
and boil afternoon sun like a gun.
A blindness of sudden familiarity then
pinned behind "Caution Horses!" I think
of Koestler and other books to re-read — what a price.

A vulture settles on roadside remains,
Bailieboro, Monaghan, Bewdley.
The clown signals "Shop Here" or "Rattan!"
Painted bright yellow bricks, a bailiwick
in the dead of winter in nineteen fourteen
that parish graveyard was not yet full,
soon it will weather winter once again — with stalks fallen.

The fair-haired hay marks rows this way
then that, over the next rise, surprise
at the passing truck now head on,
I slow and it tucks back in deference.
Who stoped here? Summer Gothic updated.
Niagara plums so cheap and ripe and
Rice Lake glows as green as a traffic light — go then.

Widow's Walk

Beyond the ceiling's plaster, a Widow's Walk —
a dormer that framed all hope and the Lake
widthways through rainstorm, snow squall, summer heat
She'd grip at a memory, his cracked lip,
a crease of dry blood, and hold. Once more, their bed
was re-made — her corners taut, slipcases ironed —
the floor broomed, salt cod held in cold water,
four flowers from the garden in a vase. There.

A silent hope of motherhood, passed down
as the Sunday pearls she unfastens, cups,
trickles into a velvet box. Powdering
in the mirror, she suspects, finally,
there must be something wrong with this watching.
She no longer longs. It is he who is lost
at sea — drowned, unburied. And she, she is bored.

The Shore

I

Shore break stirs and folds its shallow deposit, sand-clouds
storm, spit hypodermic needles and bongs (Mr. Juicy
bottles, hose, tape) at a passed-out, dropped, Bankstown slut —
final words, *Thanks for the effort*, swim inside her headache.
She'd been knackered, fell right here in the sand with a cake
of surfboard wax stuck up her, Paddle Pop sticks for ability,
the return half of a wet train ticket, crusting zinc-creamed
mouth and bloody nose. Silence. Nothing really, nothing yet.

II

The white elephant, a church on the Kingsway, kick-starts
belief like heat from that pinched, torched Torana ditched
in Kurnell late last night, bells and smoke rise in waves
filling the Shire air, not far from where Captain Cook first
stepped ashore —
     called this land, in English, English.
Then cockneys and Irish chipped in, dreaming of Australian
rules, egalitarianism, indigenous immigration laws, meat
pies, clever slang for a woman's body and her desire
to just sit with them on a beach towel, listen to Cold Chisel —
feel sun on her stomach. Get that in t'ya. Still Sydney, still.

Where Seagulls are Local

I

I fall. More cakey snow down my jumper.
Ahead you and the others walk on, faces
down shoulders hunched hard against the sting
whipping in wet and slant off Georgian Bay.
I'm still stupid among the Ontarian.
I know that's cedar now though, that Jack pine,
can spot a piece of Shield as good as the next.
I learn through such simple confrontation.

Then you and the others look back, laughing
at me brushing myself off, *Dumb Aussie!*
The storm worsens the light, flattens details
like your look, but I know the one: you're proud
and sorry. The buckle won't give, I'm stuck.
Somewhere. Someplace where I've got it all wrong
half the time. Snow. Shoe. My incorrect self,
free as a moment, like avalanche.

II

The devastation is remote, unpopular, unclear.
The seagull is atop the shopping cart sinking
knee-deep in the Ganaraska's sludge;
run-off melt ferries bits of birch bark,
Twix wrappers, husks of salmon or steelhead
(three of four washed up, petrified, death
mere evidence of successful introduction.)
Why continue to solicit: why did I come here?

III

Spend language-formative years in the antipodes.
See the boy in the driveway practicing slap shots.
Relate to him, the way one guesses at weight,
eyeing the prerequisite effort to counteract gravity.
He misses the kiddie pool, leaned on its side
against the garage door: *the net, obviously, dad.*
Say *Puck*, and watch him snarl as if at a teacher.
Should he ever need a googly, I'm prepared.

IV

Last night: our llama's forgotten lines thrown to him
in a spit-laced bark (the teacher's voice worse
than the child's mistake.) The anonymity of the wings:
Those who can't, I mouth. Mother nods viciously.
Outside the rink, parents, cold, clutch coffees: *Judy,
yours a snake or sloth?* The inhale of blue smoke,
plumes of breath condensing, disappearing into night,
mis-assigning human qualities to gods and animals alike.

V

Our ill-refined accents give us up. We laugh —
a couple of menu polyglots ordering
in the original pretension, saved by numbers
if things stray too far from urbane. Then what?
Mouthfuls of Korean your hair flicked, wrist exposed —
Where are the others, do you know?
I, the Gulf Stream counts for something.
You, insist on this Lake Effect business.

Then, a word I have never pronounced.
I conjure my brother's Australian voice, hear
him say it before I dare. I am losing overall.
Whole armies howl now on Bloor. The flags
of six foreign countries: Seoul must be alive,
cavalcades in Istanbul and Dakar. Of this we speak:
nothing matters for the next hour. The city —
beguiling ancient cultures into utter diversity.

VI

This is where our town of red trucks comes into it.
Driving alongside my half-Ridgeback, the wind
in his jowls, we pass Ontarians drinking Labatt's 50
in their driveways, without downtown irony.
Someone's got to do it. Make plastic, refine uranium.
The Plant glows green, toxic, a monotonous thrum
leaches out a throaty set of resolved atmospherics.
You are my siren, all love is made under threat.

VII

A rotten sleeper, oily and black falls away
from the Victorian viaduct, free, suicidal,
to the pavement below with a skull-like thud.
The freight, impervious, continues to loose ends
of a supply chain. Do the MBA's on computers
see the fields, lakeshores, KFC's, subdivisions,
young ones fucking under its belly, their keystrokes?
Do they account for such a stunning fall?

VIII

The preservation is near, popular, particular.
Road by road, houses have scrollwork
faithfully sanded, gingerbread restored,
brass plaques mounted affirming an authenticity
by year, builder, investment. Is fortune bilked
at another's blade or spade? We drift along
sidewalks, imagine in old glass and throw pillows.
Make nice please, pretend properly or not at all.

Via the Mine

The carriage squeals, grinds, then halts alongside
a milky green gaping vowel of a mine.
A rock cut wound; a raw entrance exposed,
our super conductor knows in passing
why we are here; what failed signals mean.
In and out of Quebecois, her two-way
conveys staccato accents, need filters
here coffee Canada Dry forty-eight.

Then sun breaks up a cloud, paradise anew
as a turquoise gauze of postcard sky heals
what was lanced, let, and a weeping eyesore.
Beyond the lips a call for a last swim,
to drown in those shallows, to wish wreckage,
the ache of gravity, minds so inclined.

The Price is the Price

The young dad, black head of hair,
thick forearms, and a dense moustache,
pushes today's silver scooter through

the Wal-Mart aisles, past the rows
of shower curtains and woks, olive oil,
automobile shampoo, Easter eggs.

He bends low, leading it away mindfully
as if a goat. The lad can hardly stand it,
can hardly keep still —

the pink wheels faux chrome, he skips
and shakes and wiggles. The mom
follows steps behind, her mouth, veiled

as the dad haggles by gesture.
The Associate: "The price is the price."
I see them again later in the food court,

sit next to them, eavesdrop, their strange
language. She is not happy, I conclude.
Silent, as a voice message interrupts

a blameless Diva. They eat elegantly.
He drinks a coffee, struggling, lid flap,
buying time — the dissonance of wants.

Now she's still, maddened. Meanwhile
the boy sits, stands, fidgets, sits, grips
the neck of the scooter, whispers to it —

he will love it forever. That moment I hear
words as they do, the boy's light, unbroken
voice carrying Canadian, their own brand

new second language, worry along with them:
who is he becoming here,
     what have we already done?

Crowd of Two

"Achtung!" The La Perouse bus rocks
the distant eucalyptus and bitumen gleam —

up close, he kills time, rubbish-abundant blue bins
unite worker bees quarrying the lemonade tack.

Submerged inside headphones, dousing what awaits
with loudness, you've drowned the idea of him

with the live version — a Düsseldorf stadium roaring
for encores, escape, bliss, meaning, pertinence. More.

All the while he only skims, too aware of the growing
swarm to call it reading. A peacekeeper on leave,

you will step off the bus and together we shall —
He suspects, they shall walk to Maroubra, or sit,

or eat scallops. And in the morning, together
you line her birdcage with the Herald, then beachcomb

the cold-cold sand, and collect cuttlefish for its beak,
pumice for coarse heels, and concave shells which later,

after love, he holds up to your ear and asks, Can you hear
the sea? And you flee into a swarm of young Germans.

Gravel, air brakes, bees — he waves, standing at ease.

A Confidential Morphology

Plastic bags snagged in tree branches.
Yard gnomes, tropical aquariums.
Mt. Rushmore, the Suez Canal.

Tractors, razors, anchors, topiary,
Glass, carbon, snails, rats,
Pork bellies, Corn Flakes,
Insane asylums, ring barking,
Soapstone, soap, honey
Sting, back burning,
Candles, paper, balloons,
Grandfathering, sunset clauses,
Igloos, Canberra, plantations,
Creationism, Greenpeace,
The sublime, the stars,
The prodigy, the Occident,
The pathetic fallacy, the Hoover.

Cars sunken at the bottom of inlets.
Oyster farms, nudist colonies.
Felt as moss in kindergarten realism.

Douglas Fir

This hill, twists and ice-slick, is no place for a Corolla.
Somehow we make it to the Douglas Fir, in rows,
as if advancing into the blades of the irritable hoards

wielding chainsaws, housedogs, bundled children.
Later, I'm at the recipe for my family's pudding,
circa 1890s Scotland and having survived a century

of fiddling in Australia — calls for dry fruit by the pound
that I mince and cut until I take the top off my thumb.
After, faint, I sip rum, see baby Jesus float past on a flatbed.

There is no snow, the sky is late light, cloud-pressed gold
and green with nothing left but an agreeable covet for tinsel,
someone's baby girl in a velvet dress to be the angel.

All mouth the archaic words, tunes flowering like paper whites
from hidden speakers in chain stores, ra pa pa pum!
My family's boozy pudding. What happened to crackers,

those paper crowns inside? The blood throbs about my cut.
I crave the torrent of explanations at gift giving. It's peace,
of a kind. Absent. Minded. Negotiated with each present.

Chelmsford Avenue

On the verandah, a young boy
could hide inside vast pottery
vases, memorizing, imagining
distinctions in the low-tide air.

At the foot of her garden
the head of a rusted pick
pokes up through the soil
anchoring plants with wire.

On the floor in the garage
slaters crawl about beneath
the purple cardboard bubbles
that once cushioned oranges.

You can try to make smooth
cement by mixing wet sand
and dirt together with a stick
in a bucket. It won't set. Ever.

Black Cloth

On the stool the sitter shifts into new hitches —
blind spots, the bifocals are flash repellent,

tie adrift, sweat beads, shadows enlarge nostrils.
If I could just move the sun an hour forward,

rotate the building fifteen degrees,
restore twenty-twenty sight

to those fifty-year-old eyes —
roam Chinatown snapping fruit

held aloft in mid-barter —
the grizzly whorls of a drunk's yellow, unclipped beard —

young boys in tight, white T-shirts
touching each other innocently, or flagrantly

over espresso, or European beer —
shoot saris on sale filling in the breeze

like a fleet of spinnakers —
pizza shops alive now it's midnight

with eleventh-hour effort and eager mouths —
telephone poles in retreat —

or the 4 a.m. rain scattering the red and green light
on the streetcar tracks

(Black cloth hung only softens May)
showing them slick and parallel and empty.

Rain

Hoofprints in muck, a thousand sure beats,
silent as the mouths of deer tracking down
the same path the wind itself takes
between sumach, cedar; width enough
as they commute, snorting and grazing,

along riverbank, around lake, across gully,
over ditch, through puddle. Blueprints
of how the land is to be tracked
and marked by Indians, traders, children
of the first farmers, and later boys

out being boys on a Sunday morning
after church; walking the tracks between
villages to catch a trout or else a girl
they fancy and might one day marry.
Orange vests survey, make a gridwork

of prime locations; Head Office books
contractors whose beepers hum promises
of work, economic renewal, as backhoes
arrive to make the earth rational, flat.
Muck clings to the bucket's teeth.

It's been raining for days now.

Hostage Hostel

How each heave counted for something like art
or a baguette, or Stella Artois, or the nine days
spent with Olga in Hostage Hostel. A whole
summer throwing bricks. And another welding
ribs into aluminium dinghies. This is in a snaking
Louvre line, and later on with beer in Minsk chasing
a Missourian, Ashley, into the White Russian night —
the weight of each brick, the tension of each rib.
Then about when Doric columns became mundane,
he chased a dry bed, antibiotics, a "square meal"
to "stick to his ribs," (neither translated into Dutch)
and the very mates he writes to, adding exclamation
marks after the Ashleys, boozey afternoons, cafés;
leaving out the bricks he heaves all the way home.

Here is my street, this tree I planted
for Raghavan, among others

You still take yourself as you used to,
the village's red dust in a dry mouth,
fashionable clothes that fit, people who

you know, knew, grew into a man with.
Familiar digs, handshakes, worn jokes,
the pout of her lip, bread that tastes like bread.
Look: here is my street, this tree I planted.

Remember when we swung on that tyre
over the flooded river and you made me
a fool in front of your sister. Damn you!

Remember that. Remember it, will you?
Wherever you are now. Bahrain, I think.
Berlin — was it then, fine. Just remember
it of a morning when you butter toast.

Last Stand of the Wollemi Pine

"The location of the pines is a secret."

I

Wollemi canopy pierced —
prehistoric whiskers

from a deep laugh line
missed by the thousand

foaming razor swipes
of sprawl, aboriginal fire-

stick farming, evolution.
Plucky, classified, alive.

II

King Billy breaks the soil during the Battle of Hastings
to find dampness, light, other editions of himself

clustered in deep cover. The leader of a band
of evolutionary exiles, humming songs of elapsed design,

left behind to their own loneliness,
genetic memories of shading great beasts.

Billy is a last war veteran, the one who recites legends —
telling what they all fought for, fled from,

how it mattered
                    at the time so many about them fell.

III

We learn on the wind Norfolk pines grow in California.
The sandstone cliff-top wears away in the heat and salt breeze.

Direct light steals further down the adjacent gorge wall.
Each year it grows hotter. There is nowhere left, only progress.

We hunker. On good nights, we have the American dream.
We await extinction. We are a hermaphroditic clone.

The eucalypts will rib:
It was a blessing. They were not themselves, in the end.

They are, though, too young to account for us,
our nameless conifer company, modish sway, abundance.

Far above we eye the forest, its traffic — sassafras
and coachwood roots work and wedge their way in,

chasing alluvium and the runoff lick. Rock splits,
along sedimentary layers. Erosion is erasure.

IV

First, their colour: wrong green.
And odd shape. Leaves like fern sprays.
Taller than trees here ought to be.

The sound changes, air at a standstill
as a cone is handled, bark palmed,
fingers dragged, bumping across

the rough of it. That was the first
(tender does it) touch.
Outclassing Banks, his mates reckon —

from that moment on, bloke in footy
shorts, professional bushwalker,
begot *Wollemia noblis*.

V

Thousands of tiny Wollemi pines
now grow in perfect rows inside

a subdivision of temperature-
controlled greenhouses,

premature babies in isolation units,
they may sense aberration —

they were not supposed to make it.
They would scream in protest,

demand death, if it were not so
beautiful here. Perhaps, they reason,

we are now in good hands,
and too young to know any better.

Notes & Acknowledgements

The author would like to acknowledge the financial support of the Ontario Arts Council through the Writers' Reserve program.

◆

The quotation by Edward Hopper is from Heinz Liesbrock's introduction "The Silent Truth of Light: Edward Hopper's Oeuvre" from, *Edward Hopper: Forty Masterworks*, Schirmer's Visual Library, W.W. Norton, 1988.

The line "Well so long, Mister, till we meet again" beginning "Stripped Fitter for the Outing" is from A.B. 'Banjo' Paterson's poem "A Disqualified Jockey's Story."

The line "The location of the pines is a secret" beginning "Last Stand of the Wollemi Pine" is from *The Wollemi Pine* by James Woodford, Text Publishing, 2002.

◆

"Roman Road" is for an old friend, John Bank, and first appeared in the *Queen Street Quarterly*. "The Dope," "The Shore," and "Hostage Hostel" first appeared in Jennifer Lovegrove's stunning handmade journal, *dig*. "The Otonabee Poems" first appeared in a different form in the art catalogue: *Jim Reid: Terraforms*, Art Gallery of Peterborough, 2001. "Measure Twice" is for E.S.G. Morgan. "Last Stand of the Wollemi Pine" was a finalist for *ARC* magazine's 2003 "Poem of the Year."

◆

I would like to thank Michael Holmes at ECW Press for his confidence and editorial guidance; and John Degen, Adam Levin, Scott Pound, and especially George Murray for sound advice, encouragement and friendship.